Branches Doubled Over with Fruit

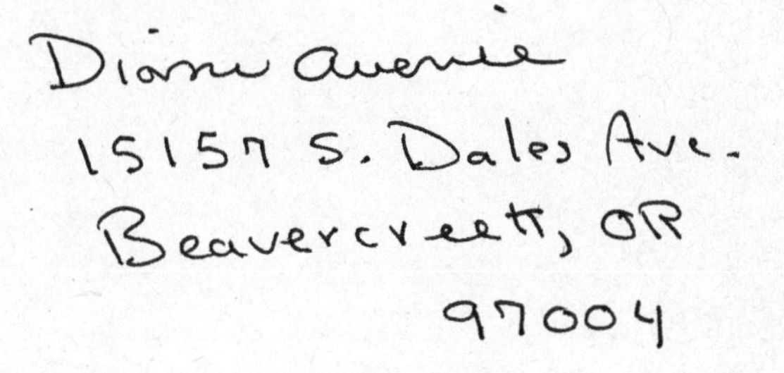

Branches Doubled Over with Fruit

Poems by

Diane Averill

University of Central Florida Press
Contemporary Poetry Series
Orlando

Printed in the U.S.A. on acid-free paper ♾

Library of Congress Cataloging-in-Publication Data

Averill, Diane.
Branches doubled over with fruit : poems / by Diane Averill.
p. cm. — (Contemporary poetry series)
ISBN 0-8130-1033-0 (cloth).
ISBN 0-8130-1034-9 (paper)
I. Title. II. Series: Contemporary poetry series (Orlando, Fla.)
PS3551.V373B7 1991
811′.54—dc20 90-21096
CIP

University Presses of Florida is the central agency for scholarly publishing of the State of Florida's university system, producing books selected for publication by the faculty editorial committees of Florida's nine public universities. Orders for books published by all member presses should be addressed to University Presses of Florida, 15 NW 15th Street, Gainesville, Florida 32611.

This book is for my daughter, Laura, and my son, Brian.
They grew up with it.

Acknowledgments

Acknowledgment is made to the following publications for poems that originally appeared in them:

Calyx: "Music Lover"
Calapooya Collage: "Grounding My Daughter"
Colorado Review: "A Woman and Two Birds"
Cutbank: "Dreams, Garbage"
Hubbub: "Fishermen at Kajikasawa"
Kalliope: "Listening to Mahler in the Kitchen," "While Moving"
Midwest Quarterly: "Leaf Tongues," "The Soil Wants Us," "Ella's Son Brings Her Gifts from Riverview Cemetery," "Firefly," "When the Wild Geese Move Past the Mercantile in a Long Body, Dancing," "When Mother Receives Gentlemen Visitors"
Mississippi Mud: "Four Thoughts on His Last Lover," "To My Daughter, Hunting Snakes," "Weeding"
Northwest Review: "Notes from Oaks Bottom Trail"
Plexus: "Heliotropic"
Poet & Critic: "Bow, horsehair"
Portland Review: "Walking the Rails"
Room of One's Own: "Grounding My Daughter," "Keeping Distance"
Seattle Review: "After Breaking with Ben, Ella Receives a Postcard from Him, August 3, 1914," "Ella Sees Those Maps Her Son's Fingers Make on Her Walls," "Feathers"
Sinister Wisdom: "Center for Delinquent Girls"
Tar River Poetry: "Steps in Composition: Four Students"
Three Rivers Poetry Journal: "Bad for You," "Renewal"

I would like to thank Ann Bailey, Molly Bellman, Henry Carlile, Linda Cheney, Helen Dickinson, Pamela Gonsalves, Steve Myers, Ralph Salisbury, and Joel Weinstein for their comments on this manuscript.

"The Ella Featherstone Poems: A Sellwood Sequence" was first published in a limited edition of one hundred copies by Howlet Press Chapbooks in January 1990.

Contents

Branches Doubled Over with Fruit

Racing Snakes

Nail polish was our first cosmetic experiment,
our way of making up with snakes
for stepping on them,
each scale a fingernail.
After we painted their tails crimson and pink
they ribboned off sideways like kitetails.
Sally and I never knew who won.

Later we let them go in woods.
Catching them again was like teasing brats.
Streetfighters of the forest,
we'd feel them tremble in our fingers
and twist like braids in rubber bands.

When prissy Mrs. Cooper scolded us
for cutting across her lawn
I tucked a silky garter
in my training bra and touched
her brass monster knocker.
She opened, I shook my tee shirt
and the snake slithered out
of the stiff cotton cup.

Mrs. Cooper's face was that orange,
Sunday-school-magazine hue
of one who'd witnessed the supernatural.
A blue vein jumped out of my skin,
scribbled on the welcome mat
and cut across her grass.

Bow, horsehair

I searched for the scent of sweat,
wanting horses,
but Mother was metronome,
her hands allegro on faucets.

I practiced, keeping the mute on rosewood,
hands loose on the silver bridle of evening.
I rode past fern-thin curtains,
a neck turning, dark, under my palm.

The Ornament

(after *Mother and Child*—Mary Cassatt)

Mother holds me up
in a mirror.
My body bends, a stem
in the glass
as she presses me to her lap.

We rock in the tight
green of a chair.
My gold hair spreads in petals.
Hers winds back on itself,
stored ribbon above her face.
We wait for Father.

Mother is proud of me—
my face a sunflower
pinned to her dress,
my eyes brown as bees
crawling in the center.

Starting the Curse

The summer my tree
first raised peaches
Father propped sticks under
branches doubled over with fruit.
I strained to reach robin's eggs—
blue buttons cracked on my shirt.

I held tea that seemed to bleed
in the cup, waited
while my clothes spun the machine.
My fingers pulled wicker from lawn chairs—
on Mother's legs, veins broke.

Feathers

The hours pull apart.
The hands that pull feathers apart
are children's. They gather
the arches of feathers
in cardboard boxes,
gather the colors of feathers,
storing them in the garage
while they play out.

The feathers can't start
because they are no longer
with their bodies. They wait
like old sighs glowing.

They listen to the children's voices
leaking through cracks in the door.
Scrapings of old spoons,
pocketknives planting shriveled tops
of carrots by the side of the garage.

The children leave,
their voices trailing.
The hands of children will come back.
They will come pulling feathers.

Keeping Distance

When Mother stopped giving you
her thin ribbons of milk,
I pulled on your baby blanket
'til it gave. You carried its slippery
satin bindings for years,
calling them your "corners."

Taller than you,
I had to feed our goldfish
their daily pinch.
Yours rose to the top,
belly up,
a pattern wrong side out.

This morning
from my half-open window,
sister, you are a curtain trailing me
deep in my room. Tears
unravel from your eyes like satin threads.
You ask for help
but my hands feel full of hooks.

Better keep your distance,
sister, back away like the daytime
moon, its bruises only haze.
Aesthetic. And out of my reach.

Notes from Oaks Bottom Trail

An hour shaped for walking. Rain, then mist.
Rain's not different from mist, but it has direction.
A day I will not call schizophrenic. A thing that varies
gets bad names. I left Brian playing Limbo under a grape
arbor shingled with leaves. His friend turns the hose on
long while Brian backbends under a rope of water. Each
time he gets by, the rope goes lower. Last night he had a
question. The question was, "I'm scared." When he saw
Jaws, I wanted to tell him sharks aren't real, like the
ghosts. He put masking tape on windows, kept them out.
I told him sharks live deeper then we do, can't come on
land. He said they can if they bring a hose. We make
trails for our fears to find us. The oak tree on this
trail seems artificial. Created by Maxfield Parrish.
A way he had of polishing the leaves with light. Someone
broke a tree for fire, left two logs lying in the curls
of moss. There's so much growth here the creek shows
small, tame as a pocket mirror. Women have no wilderness
in them, Louise Bogan wrote; yet lying in the cool
vibrato of these long grasses, the blades of my body
turn easily and children's lives grow from me like thorns.
When Brian was still young enough to remember power,
he'd wrap his legs around my hip, point where he wanted
to be, then lift a finger to the moon, tell me "turn
it off." Above, the maple tree is calm as a good parent.
My breaths are longer here, not piled on top of each
other. Later, I'll bring Brian yellow leaves
to light his sleep.

Weeding

After the quarrel, my pear tree goes pale
as an ice storm, destructive with flowers.
The phone curls against the porch, stubborn
root of our talk, as I weed the afternoon.
Cineraria glows in dirt, each bloom a red knuckle.
I pull grass from the anxious faces of pansies,
add to the long body of compost.
Various strains of daffodil grow tight
in corners like separate convictions.

When light takes its last step across my back,
I go in, wash my son's hair over the sink.
His small nakedness concentrates on a towel—
wet strands tangle in my fingers like weeds.
He pulls away, then we're separate, the way lovers are
separate on the phone, words severed from touch.

Letter from a Wrought Iron Porch

(to Helen)

I smooth the sheets, tuck them under the
clipboard, move words around. Above the wrought iron leaves
fencing this porch, the sky rearranges its clouds. I hold
the pen tight, my life getting a good grip on me. The phone
rings—Joe. Tells of a man trying to break a world record.
Thirty-four days locked in a room with poisonous snakes.
No known antidotes. Been there thirteen. The night power
went off snakes huddled against him for warmth. Men make it
hard on themselves. The telephone wraps its red cord around
my arm. Branches break into networks along the sky like the veins
on my leg. Yesterday wading the river. A barge carrying crushed
rocks passed right after a locomotive rushed with lumber.
Both broken loads and me in the middle listening to identical
horns. Scotch broom pushed yellow flowers on the bank.
"Lover gone" is always part of the landscape, concealed at
first like those dot-to-dot pictures my son connects in
kindergarten. Backyard summers, my best friend and I jumped
from swings at the top of the arc. We placed sticks where
our toes landed to see where we were. You remind me of walking
barefoot in wet sand. How I made prints, then backed
over them, confusing people into thinking steps end nowhere.
Helen, we'll always be wading knee deep in each other's lives.
Yesterday after the river, I walked to a conference at school
past flowering plums. Blossoms sift down, roll on yellow
lines in the Thriftway parking lot, like chalkdust falling
from long erasers I banged together when it was my turn for
cleaning. Mrs. Cooper divided the world into math and grammar,
as we divide the world into poems and lovers. On a bush
outside the dead glass of school, leaves redden. Roses copy color.
I'm sending you two paperbacks, underlined. Love, Diane.

Her Spiritual Education

In spring I tie
stems of lavender with night-
colored thread, hang two
bunches upside down like bat wings
over Laura's cradle.

Grandfather wants her
in church but
mornings when she reaches for the strong
blue wind-
chimes I placed over her sleep,
Laura pulls on them to wake me
then pulls on me for milk
and we listen instead to lavender's
many-scented voices.

To My Daughter, Hunting Snakes

You stalk,
feet bare as leaves,
wanting to know
copperheads or rattlers,
swift as your brown hair
sliding in light.

They hide in grass where paths
fork, coiled in sun.
Lock on one.
Squeeze it with your palm.

As you carry it home
over the stones,
concentrate on the quick tongue.
Do not turn to watch
red petals drop.

Grounding My Daughter

At night
the lost boys hang upside down
from the rafters of the garage.
When they wave their wands of
mascara, pistils quiver
in my flower bed. My daughter
combs her blue hair. She
decorates her fingers
with spiders.

I double-bolt our door,
but there is nothing
I can do about the bat voices
that slip through the phone,
turning her cheeks geranium.

Center for Delinquent Girls

In a dirt-dark room
suitcases glow in rows.
Folded flowers. Snapdragons.
Sun's locked outside like a pimp.
At odd angles to each other,
some suitcases look like
broken limbs.

At the Glass Club last June
Deanna watched people
dance the Black Lint.
She'd go home. Practice. Come back.
But each time
the dance had changed.
She never danced there.
Here, Deanna can't talk
to Linda. Each with a record
of prostitution, caught
in a plot to run.
At night they dance to records,
mirror each other, practice.

On dish duty, one girl turned
the sprayer on Susan
to see her breath quicken
to watch her
small breasts swim
under the wet blue
surface of her teeshirt.
Outside on smoke break
the girls play ring-around-the rosy,

circle the girl who sprayed Susan.
They sing and link
arms like a wire fence.

Teresa sits alone,
smoke webbing her face.
Teresa keeps a dream
journal. Always dreams
in color. White
lines on the black top
remind her of cocaine.
"Can't cross those lines."
Beyond, the fence
seems painted on
landscape, a prop.
"Some girls scale it when they run."

Wind blows the leaves
of the sunburst locust
so far to the right
the trunk begins to spin.
Ashes ashes we all fall down.
But the girls keep singing.

Colors

Instructions for tie-dying
glide around the back
porch steps, catch
in blue-green weeds
grown from thrown-out
cockatiel seed.
Stars splay out
like white cotton
released from rubber
bands into the growing
dark. Excitement spreads
around the knots in Jim's
voice, calling "rad."
Days ago, his father turned
him out, "for good."

White-knuckled with bands,
one of the shirts waits
like a fist. Julie stands
arms dead-bolted
against her chest.
Julie couldn't have
her school picture taken—
her father stained her
cheek a blue-yellow bruise.
His knuckled anger
threw her things
in the yard with Jim's—
pom-poms and koala bear.
"Just another massacre father,"
says the daughter.
She dips her new

shirt into vinegar
to hold the blues.
These are colors
she can take on
and off when she wants.

Julie's voice has knots
that never go away.
Jim's voice smooths out
as he spreads his shirt
on the line
under the bare bulb of the moon.

Julie shows her fake
fingernails, tells of Rob,
a born-again
model for men's magazines.
"Can you tell which ones
are real? These will do
until the new ones grow."
Rob gives her money
for Jim.

White moths drift in
and out among the weeds.
Something seems
erased from their wings.

Steps in Composition: Four Students

i.
"Three years I spend in Thailand refugee camp.
There was no books and no paper."
This is an example of a lack
of agreement.

ii.
"If I don't get laid pretty soon
I'm going to murder somebody, how does that grab you."
You need
a question mark here, as this is a direct
rather than an indirect question.
Your other error is
the comma splice.

iii.
A run-on sentence is an even greater error
than a comma splice, as it implies
that the writer does not sense
a pause between two complete thoughts.
"My four year old child was murdered by a sicko
I thought was my friend I went crazy for awhile"
is a run-on. What you need here is
a period.

iv.
Kathy uses a period
when she writes,

"I was thirteen when I finally got my father
to quit molesting me by threatening him with a gun."
A period is like a bullet between two
thoughts. Everything comes to
a complete stop.
Now, see if you can start a new paragraph.

Dreams, Garbage

When the dreams began
crowding potatoes and beans
from the counter,
you dropped them in the garbage
among banana peels slippery as foreskin,
the wet news. The garbage lid's
clamped tight as a migraine.
The house is tidy. But someone has
framed your arm in oak,
tacked it above the couch.
And your breasts, those two dachshunds,
nose against your blouse,
trying to get out, trying
to stop the cat's tongue
from licking away your ankles,
your legs disappearing like milk.

Heliotropic

Isn't it funny she says
motioning toward the side yard,
how the children cut off the heads of sunflowers
making a tent with the stalks.
Her pool's a snapshot of the sky.
We sit on the grass surrounding it
like a page in an album,
looking at the captured sun
skewered by a power line.
I drink lemonade and admire her house,
pasted at all four corners to its lawn.
She brings me photos from Great Falls.
The family, interspersed in rows of sunflowers.
Faces turn in unison toward the father,
his perfect finger on the shutter.
In one shot, she holds the youngest up
to a sunflower curled at the edges,
beautiful as a sea anemone ready to close.

Walking the Rails

The wives walk out under the white-grey sky
with one blue scratch across it.
For one hour, arms horizontal
they play on rails to keep balance.
They look down at cracked wood of ties
while poplar leaves turn silver sides to the wind.

They talk of the summer they were twelve,
taking lunches into the fall,
naming each other. Hobo. Tinker.
How they'd traveled:
pissing over mossy rocks,
crouching in forts baled into hay
where light came through in needles,
bringing water to the eyes.

At home, there are tables to set.
But they continue down rails,
talking of men who are not husbands,
who rushed into their lives
like the heads of trains, or like
turning a corner back to twelve.
Find the real hobo, camped by a dead fire
where the night before, flames hummed
halfway up the log, persistent as yellow jackets,
then stopped.

The Mother

Once, an ecosystem of young girls
grew from a room off my kitchen.
Planted too close together,
some leaned into wallpaper and disappeared,
others branched out the window
blooming rock music.

This spring the last two
leapt from the second story.
One laughed like lilac under wet purple skies,
the other blew away in a strong
breeze the way apple blossoms
cover the garden beds. For awhile,
I couldn't see the weeds.

Their old dog died last week.
Now, when I turn the burning
log in the woodstove, an orange alligator
sleeps by my bed, friendly but
untouchable. Fire curls

like the fern in the corner,
an adolescent maidenhair that moved with me
into the small studio;
one last daughter. Its green
arms turn like the hands
on the clock above it,
grandmother's, that kept her to school
on time, back in 1907.
It still tells the truth, snaps each

minute to my attention the way pitch snaps
inside the fire.

Late at night I wake to white
ash, dark coal, a black
and white photo of my favorite
daughter. She changed form
like the burning
fir, returns to me
over the phone,
her voice ornamental as smoke.

While Moving

We talk of men and the way glass
cracks in cold. Like a white
wicker chair on the porch in snow.
And there is more
snow falling on the white wicker.
The move from your house to the small
studio is like walking in black
high heels in snow. We are
forest-colored eyes, an arrangement
of orange pekoe tea and women.
We toss a picture of your lover
before he broke with you.
We talk of saving
a pane for its pattern,
for the way glass cracks.
"We're friends because we like the same
surfaces." Chocolate wafers on a white
plate. After the break, you divided music.
It was then he mentioned custody,
slipping the talk between album covers.
He wants the White Album, he wants
custody of the snow.

(for Ann Bailey, painter)

Shifting Landscapes

At Ann's house
watercolors form membranes
between kitchen, studio and bedroom
so you have
to be careful of the silver
wire whip as it passes
from hand to hand over the bowl
until cream slides slick.
This can realign her childhood
hills of Wisconsin
leaving too much
white space over the farm.

She has no
cat that scratches
and claws the green
upholstery of paint
but when her lover takes
her tongue on a long journey
of brush strokes
it changes the direction of acrylic—
red deepens in the skin
of the Mandela portrait.
Back in Wisconsin
there are sudden faces all over
the lean magenta grasses.

Fishermen at Kajikasawa

(after a painting by Hokusai)

Mt. Fuji's a line, a hook into
mist delicate as memory.
Sun's a gesture,
a stain in the air.

Bent with the
efforts of spiders, fishermen
stand on a green rib of land,
a hard wave. Long lines
spin from fingers to water.
The ocean fights back
with white claws,
with a wave that pulls away
like an answering argument.

Or, the men aren't
fishermen, they're riders
of that blue horse, the ocean,
and the lines are green reins
of tension, a form of seaweed.

A Woman and Two Birds

She crawls under the warm
veins of her electric blanket,
turns controls,
while black ice seals the ground
shut against birds.
All fall she fed them sunflower seeds,
so they never flew
south, taking their colors
from her trees.

Now, their sharp cries
rise to the arc light,
catch in her window prism,
that cold eye of night
dangling on its worm-like thread.
Half asleep inside the black pane
she waits for the sharp
beaks, their small dependencies.

Two Women in the Mall after the Seventh Mt. Saint Helens Eruption

Already bored with the bad news the mountain
puts out, few people wear masks.
We wonder how long it will take
for the new ash to reach us, as if we were
discussing faults in the postal system.
Steam puts out new blossoms in distance. The blue
hydrangea rocks in its bowl between us.
I drink scullcap tea. You sip gin from cut glass.

You say ash is good for your garden. You say
you let your cucumbers go too far this year.
I watch a woman bent
holding purse to shoes,
shopping for the perfect match. The sun dulls.
You light a cigarette, take out a letter from
your lover. Obsidian slips out of the letter.
Smoke curls around your arm
like an expensive bracelet,
then unclasps you, becomes part of the light.
You lean on the light, ask if replying
to his statements with honest ones
can get you a compromise,
the way squash crossbreeds in your garden.
You say ash is good for your garden.
I want to go outside. A woman near us
tries on wild silk blouses, the cracks in her
face covered with fine powder.

The Soil Wants Us

(after Tranströmer)

Spring, and the soil
wants us to plant our sadness
so it may bloom lilac tears.

In summer, the soil
wants us to unwind the wisteria from our hearts
so the potato bugs can uncurl their silver chambers.

By fall the soil
wants us to place deadly nightshade berries
in bowls that say "for decorative use only"
in memory of women who widened their pupils
with poison.

It is winter now, and the soil
wants us to see that the reflection
of the full moon is a pupil
widened in the eye of the lake.
It waits for men to fall
into its white-gold well.

Four Thoughts on His Last Lover

i.
I was innocent with her. "Be careful,"
she warned, "or you'll end up the missing
child on the back of a milk carton."

ii.
Once we were hiking in the gorge. Senses
opened out to seventeen scents, all of them
wet. We climbed Beacon Rock together in an
effortless spiral, reaching the top the same
time as a hawk. But when she plucked the fringe
from her blue shawl, feathers began falling
from the hawk's wings.

iii.
She held my head in her hands, tapped
it lightly against the edge of her bowl until
it cracked, then gathered all my best thoughts
and put them in an herb jar. She placed that
jar on her windowsill, labeled, in alphabetical
order, along with thoughts of her other
lovers, present and past. The sun penetrated
first through her window, then through
the glass jar, until my thoughts lost all
their fragrance and potency.

iv.
Arms Are For Hugging, says her sticker.
But don't you believe it. The whole
world is losing its immune system and
beautiful lovers are like holding healing crystals.
They can't protect anyone. And now you want me to love you?

Bad for You

You think I am
some strange pesticide
sleeping against your skin.
You think a woman
offering herself
is a poisoned apple.

You want me
to make you decaf
espresso. You ask for
popcorn, no
butter, no sex.

You think I want
to crouch like this
along your perfect
silk arteries of
fear all night?
You think I want to be
the gargoyle of your heart?

Rhubarb Morning

You are a light
green sword of rhubarb
that pokes its way out
still attached
to the coiled black
umbilical
of last year's plant.

I feel myself
halfway between
plant and sky
around your rhubarb morning.
When I hug you I close
my eyes. Forsythia
blooms on the lids.

Music Lover

Tonight the moon
is so loud
I almost told it
to quiet down
because I know you'd rather
we lie under the blue
weather of the piano.
Turn off the music and listen.
The many-tongued coleus
is full of advice,
not all of it gossip.
Or, you could start
with the hard, clear dialect
of that cut-glass necklace,
then listen to the rumors
of its neighbors,
those black silk scarves.
Look at them
unfiltered by music
and they will tell you
what they know.
Now look at me.

Coda

A young robin
from the open
double doors of the store
hops on the free
papers, cocks its head
to eye the black
worms of print
in the *Village Voice.*
Its parent calls from the walk,
but the bird answers to Scriabin,
spins deeper in.

Yesterday driving
home from the breakup
I hit the stopped
traffic, then looked.
The street went straight up
in the air broken
for a ship—
the Burnside Bridge.

I have lost all sense
of direction.
I don't know
the difference between
in and music,
love or stop.

Listening to Mahler in the Kitchen

Covering the sole with olive oil and herbs,
he slides it into the blue baking dish,
touches her with his finger tips,
leaving a light scent of rosemary on her cheeks.
The shadows of a sunburst locust reach
through parted curtains. Wood shadows
are not quite human. Still, they are
little tongues along her bare back.
He reaches for a lemon, and cupping
its small hardness in one hand, slices
through its light, puts his fingers
in his mouth, sucking tart juices.
Reaching up, he pulls the curtains closed.
A knife of light slices through the Mahler.
She feels split off from him.
From the lemon and the music.
She goes to a tall oak stool and sits
and watches the two halves of bright fruit
in the dark. He doesn't see her now.
Intent on rolling the lemon between
his fingers, he squeezes it over the fish.
The shadows are shut out but some sun still
comes from cracks in the curtains,
making slice marks on his bare chest.
This hurts her. He seems not to feel.
He is self-contained as the spices in jars.
He is contained in the Mahler.
He winds around the room, a needle doing
slow curves in the music, doing the dark.
But she reopens the curtains,

lets leaf shadows back in
as he opens the oven for fish.
He. She. Do shadows have gender? Yes.
But they resemble each other anyway.

Renewal

In the light falling from old growth trees
I saw Salamander, a burning ember
and here with you at Oceanside Cafe
this is like the swirls of red in your dark beard.
The sun has walked on your skin, set fire to it.
I ask about red-headed relatives.
When you say Grandfather
I see all the way back
before he surfaces in your eyes.

Salamander swam in the creek
but on land he was a slow
flow over red bark
turning back
to earth. He moved aside
to let me pass on the trail
but I sat down with him
the way I sit with you now
in this cafe. Love is war, you say.
No? What is it then?

Salamanders mate slowly, under water.
But you never took your
shoes off on the sand.

I sat with Salamander on
red logs, thoughts breaking down
into earth and we
looked at each other
out of different eyes, curious
and trusting. You and Renardo talk
about women, Ann and I about men,

and though you and I also talk of men and women
we can't convey the differences in talk.

But there is harmony here,
and grace, the swimming of our thoughts together
that of lizards with soft skins,
where love renews itself
in light growing
tips, and is different
colors further back.
Love is more than war.
It sets fire to our skin,
brings hidden selves to surface.

In Your Senses

Under the pale arm of the daytime
moon bent at the elbow
I turn a corner around your arm
and find myself
walking through you, still
as this summer air.
I want to play in you.
I am the quiet aggressor.
You quiver with silver webs.
When I fall apart you catch
me, a berry petal
swinging light.

There are layers of
voices in the marsh of mind.
Listen to the bird-tangle.
We swim deep,
minnows doubling ourselves with shadow—
but also the white
seeds floating the surface of each
other's skin.

We are new
as babies watching the orange
gestures of thin-skinned columbine,
the first expressions
forming on the faces of foxglove.
We are
dizzy ants crawling over old oak.

Far from the Wooden Mask of My House

This morning you are far
as those cloud feathers
that ripple the green
surface of firs in the west hills.
I watch caterpillars stroking new
leaves, remember
my fingers along your shoulders,
your back.

There are spines in this pond.
Swimming ducks send the sun colors shivering
along the water's skin, the reflected
bones of trees.

I am far from the wooden
mask of my house,
caught under spring
clouds that are sudden and close.
They move the quiet around,
opening my skin
so that it may
flower in the innocent, promiscuous rain.

Leaf Tongues

Here is the perfect green
filbert leaf. The shadow
of the one above it
curves over its leaf fur.
Its body is not perfect but
the small hole in the shadow
lets the sun drop
its bright coin through.
Your touch turns
the surface of my skin
to lake water.
You play with my colors like sun,
though neither of us
is perfect here
at the end of summer.

Open Windows

You wake to the rattle of shopping cart wheels
on the street below. It is the old woman, her cart,
her little orange flower petals that spill on top
of your stove. You wipe them off with a dishrag,
then clean the cast iron. In September you begin
to grow old. Thistle seeds falling through the
living room turn your hair white at the temples.
You close your windows.

Closed Windows

Stars no longer live in the corners of your bedroom,
spreading their spidery light. You no longer hear
the recipes of the old woman. Wrapped in burlap, she
and her belongings seem all one thing. The fishing
pole she made from a branch turned back into a blue
heron and has flown to the marsh. Brief as a
smile, summer returns each afternoon, leaving
clouds leashed to your pear tree.

The Ella Featherstone Poems: A Sellwood Sequence

(name found in a collection of old book plates)

After Mr. Featherstone's Funeral at Riverview Cemetery, March 10, 1912

Mornings,
Ella sits in the cluttered
kitchen
waiting for the shoes
to help her
find them.
When she puts them on
they're still
whispering secrets in suede.

Ella Sees Those Maps Her Son's Fingers Make on Her Walls

Evening. Moon antique. Brittle.
When her son rejects the bath,
she recalls first grade.
Water magnified the thorns,
a cut stem arched
in a vase on Miss Cooper's desk.
She was so careful she tipped it,
her map blurred.
Green for land ran into the ocean.

Ella's Son Brings Her Gifts from Riverview Cemetery

Because my fingers play
in river water
while Mother sits in her armless
rocker with only the swirls
on our oak table,
I bring her licorice fern
roots. She puts them in the clock
under the pendulum.
Next, I reach under leaf mold
for ginger blossoms.
But she brushes them off
my palm, heart-shaped leaves
still pulsing.
I offer trillium but
she plucks each white wing
from the green spine talking
of Father's death.
So the day she coils
her hair on top
I catch a garter snake
with eyes like unripe currants
then slip it inside the dresser
with her black silk stockings.

Widower Treadwell's calling cards

fall on my porch like the flat
stones my son skips on the river.

The hand mirror Treadwell gives me
belonged to his first wife.
My face slides off its bevelled
edges. She died in childbirth.

I've never had a hand mirror
I haven't broken.
They fall through my years,
backs intact as playing cards,
fronts a collection of wrinkles.

Firefly

One evening near
the red stained door
by the apple orchard
my son places
a firefly on
my wedding ring finger.

Ella's spider plant

decorates her kitchen with white flowers,
but she notices points
growing out at her
like sharp remarks.
For weeks, roots pace in circles
at the bottom of the pot.
The new thing descends
one night on her window ledge
uncurling among abalone shells.

When the Wild Geese Move Past the Mercantile in a Long Body, Dancing

My young suitor, Ben,
takes me to Spruce Run Road.
The woods come close,
make green gestures
like a shy walker.
But we bring worries,
like unfavorite jewelry,
and there are hairpin
turns in our talk—
my son's troubles accepting Ben.

When we get out of the carriage
we follow a path down
to the river.
Ben takes off some of his
clothes for a swim—
his surfaces are wet as
his paintings of grapes.
I get quiet, walk on rocks.
The air currents in this liquid green
woods want to take you with them.
They turn your thoughts over,
easy as alder leaves.
Later, we walk wooden ties
to a railroad bridge. We hold on
to wires, cross where birches
let light through
like lace. Back home, I sew
my son's clothes on the horsehair sofa
while he watches
Ben from the brocade chair.

When Mother receives gentlemen visitors

I slide into the space
between the down comforter
and the wavy wallpaper
the way my Indian head nickel
slipped down a crack
in the wooden sidewalk.

I hide under the springs
of her bed. A dust ball.
My father is not dead
he is hiding from us
in the wardrobe, the
cedar chest, or the small
yellow house over the well.

Some Lines from Evangeline under a Green Awning

Ella, she was decent,
wore high-topped shoes
with black laces.
Now she's affected.
Since that painter fella
she wears what she pleases,
those little nothin' shoes.

On Her Way to the Lavender Club Meeting Evangeline Stops to Visit Ella

I watch Ella pull the lock-stitch
on the seam of her empty flour sacks.
She washes the cotton in strong yellow
soap, opens it to the sun.
She tells me she will sew
dish towels, aprons, underwear.
"My goodness," I say. "My word,
marry Mr. Treadwell you won't
be poor." Ella looks down at
our tea. It darkens. Outside,
she turns the cloth over,
spreads the red letters
as the fast-color dye whitens
on her grass.

Ella Receives an Unwanted Guest, July 8, 1913

I sit in wicker. Spider rocks above
on her dangerous hammock in the pleasure wind
while Treadwell calls me his little
buttercup. He wobbles onto my porch
like a bumblebee,
awkward as one
of my son's huge marbles.
"Aren't you afraid at night?
I can protect you."
"I'm expecting," I say
as his alarmed eyes roll,
"a piano student."

That evening while my son sleeps
I go back out
on the porch alone,
drink licorice tea under the
moon, that quiet centerpiece of night.

Shy in beginnings, Beth

will only play the piano
if I am far from her.
She stops,
like crickets in blackberry thickets,
when I approach.

Later, she lets me place
my fingers near hers on the keys.
We slide easily over scales—
salmon over wet rocks.
When she learns "Amazing Grace"
she'll play for Sundays.

Ella Buys from the Fishmonger

Live musical notes quicken in me,
rush like bubbles in the river.
My son plays Annie Annie Over
with a friend; the rhythm of his ball
counterpoints along our roof.

When Sam, the fish peddler in his creaking
wagon, calls out "Fish, fresh fish,"
his voice pushes through my new sounds.
I remember Ben,
who will soon be here for dinner,
asking for fish.

Sam lifts the canvas curtain.
Stagnant fish eyes stare up at me
from wet gunny sacks.

All afternoon the dead music
lies with the fish on ice,
waiting for Ben.

While Dusting Family Portraits Ella Thinks of the Future

Some days
I worry about the way
light is disappearing
from my walls as
more and more of
Ben's paintings grow there.

After Breaking with Ben, Ella Receives a Postcard from Him, August 3, 1914

I would elbow through trees
to find your weekend in the park,
sell you my new revision of sunlight.
If you close your eyes to avoid me,
dreaming of two sailboats on the river,
I will hover over your eyelids
like a white moth.

Ella dreams the white moth

with adagio wings
drifts over the lid
of her
piano, which she opens
and shuts when she wants.

photo by Ancil Nance

Diane Averill was raised in Oregon, among sisters and woods. She holds an M.F.A. from the University of Oregon, where she won the annual award for the best poem by a graduate student in 1982. She taught creative writing in the Portland Public School's Talented and Gifted Program from 1983 to 1987. For the past three years, she has been teaching in the English departments at Lewis & Clark College and Portland Community College. Her two children, and her friendships with visual artists, are important sources of imagery in her poems.

University of Central Florida Contemporary Poetry Series

Diane Averill, *Branches Doubled Over with Fruit*
George Bogin, *In a Surf of Strangers*
Van K. Brock, *The Hard Essential Landscape*
Lynn Butler, *Planting the Voice*
Daryl Ngee Chinn, *Soft Parts of the Back*
Rebecca McClanahan Devet, *Mother Tongue*
Rebecca McClanahan Devet, *Mrs. Houdini*
Gerald Duff, *Calling Collect*
Malcolm Glass, *Bone Love*
Barbara L. Greenberg, *The Never-Not Sonnets*
Susan Hartman, *Dumb Show*
Lola Haskins, *Forty-four Ambitions for the Piano*
Lola Haskins, *Planting the Children*
William Hathaway, *Looking into the Heart of Light*
Michael Hettich, *A Small Boat*
Roald Hoffmann, *Gaps and Verges*
Roald Hoffmann, *The Metamict State*
Hannah Kahn, *Time, Wait*
Michael McFee, *Plain Air*
Richard Michelson, *Tap Dancing for the Relatives*
David Posner, *The Sandpipers*
Nicholas Rinaldi, *We Have Lost Our Fathers*
CarolAnn Russell, *The Red Envelope*
Robert Siegel, *In a Pig's Eye*
Edmund Skellings, *Face Value*
Edmund Skellings, *Heart Attacks*
Ron Smith, *Running Again in Hollywood Cemetery*
Katherine Soniat, *Cracking Eggs*
Dan Stap, *Letter at the End of Winter*